Pain Relievers, Diet Pills,
& Other Over-the-Counter Drugs

Junior Drug Awareness

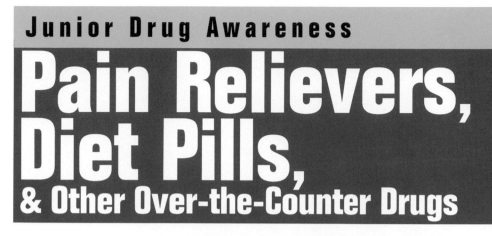

Junior Drug Awareness

Pain Relievers, Diet Pills, & Other Over-the-Counter Drugs

Introduction by **BARRY R. McCAFFREY**
Director, Office of National Drug Control Policy

Foreword by **STEVEN L. JAFFE, M.D.**
Senior Consulting Editor,
Professor of Child and Adolescent Psychiatry, Emory University

Stephen Bird

B. Joan McClure, B.N.Sc., R.N.

Chelsea House Publishers
Philadelphia

CHELSEA HOUSE PUBLISHERS
Editor in Chief Stephen Reginald
Production Manager Pamela Loos
Director of Photography Judy L. Hasday
Art Director Sara Davis
Managing Editor James D. Gallagher
Senior Production Editor LeeAnne Gelletly

Staff for PAIN RELIEVERS, DIET PILLS, AND OTHER
OVER-THE-COUNTER DRUGS
Senior Editor Therese De Angelis
Contributing Editor Elaine Andrews
Associate Art Director Takeshi Takahashi
Cover Illustrator/Designer Keith Trego
Produced by 21st Century Publishing and Communications, Inc.

Cover Photo PhotoDisc Vol. 40 #40058

The Chelsea House World Wide Web address is
http://www.chelseahouse.com

First Printing
1 3 5 7 9 8 6 4 2

Library of Congress Cataloging-in-Publication Data

Bird, Stephen.
Pain relievers, diet pills, and other over-the-counter drugs
/ Stephen Bird, B. Joan McClure.
      pp.   cm. — (Junior drug awareness)
Includes bibliographical references and index.
Summary: Describes pain relievers, diet pills, and other
over-the-counter drugs, their use in treating various health
problems, their side effects, and their dangers if misused.
ISBN 0-7910-5203-6 (hardcover)
1. Drugs, Nonprescription—Juvenile literature. [1. Drugs,
Nonprescription.] I. McClure, B. Joan. II. Title. III. Series.
RM671.A1B54 1999
615'.1—dc21   99-20186
                                                   CIP

#

by Barry R. McCaffrey
Director, Office of National
Drug Control Policy

Staying Away from Illegal Drugs, Tobacco Products, and Alcohol

Good health allows you to be as strong, happy, smart, and skillful as you can possibly be. The worst thing about illegal drugs is that they damage people from the inside. Our bodies and minds are wonderful, complicated systems that run like finely tuned machines when we take care of ourselves.

Doctors prescribe legal drugs, called medicines, to heal us when we become sick, but dangerous chemicals that are not recommended by doctors, nurses, or pharmacists are called illegal drugs. These drugs cannot be bought in stores because they harm different organs of the body, causing illness or even death. Illegal drugs, such as marijuana, cocaine or "crack," heroin, methamphetamine ("meth"), and other dangerous substances are against the law because they affect our ability to think, work, play, sleep, or eat.

If anyone ever offers you illegal drugs or any kind of pills, liquids, substances to smoke, or shots to inject into your body, tell them you're not interested. You should report drug pushers—people who distribute these poisons—to parents, teachers, police, coaches, clergy, or other adults whom you trust.

Cigarettes and alcohol are also illegal for youngsters. Tobacco products and drinks like wine, beer, and liquor are particularly harmful for children and teenagers because their bodies, especially their nervous systems, are still developing. For this reason, young people are more likely to be hurt by illicit drugs—including cigarettes and alcohol. These two products kill more people—from cancer, and automobile accidents caused by intoxicated drivers—than all other drugs combined. We say about drug use: "Users are losers." Be a winner and stay away from illegal drugs, tobacco products, and alcoholic beverages.

Here are four reasons why you shouldn't use illegal drugs:

- Illegal drugs can cause brain damage.
- Illegal drugs are "psychoactive." This means that they change your personality or the way you feel. They also impair your judgment. While under the influence of drugs, you are more likely to endanger your life or someone else's. You will also be less able to protect yourself from danger.
- Many illegal drugs are addictive, which means that once a person starts taking them, stopping is extremely difficult. An addict's body craves the drug and becomes dependent upon it. The illegal drug–user may become sick if the drug is discontinued and so may become a slave to drugs.

- Some drugs, called "gateway" substances, can lead a person to take more-dangerous drugs. For example, a 12-year-old who smokes marijuana is 79 times more likely to have an addiction problem later in life than a child who never tries marijuana.

Here are some reasons why you shouldn't drink alcoholic beverages, including beer and wine coolers:

- Alcohol is the second leading cause of death in our country. More than 100,000 people die every year because of drinking.
- Adolescents are twice as likely as adults to be involved in fatal alcohol-related car crashes.
- Half of all assaults against girls or women involve alcohol.
- Drinking is illegal if you are under the age of 21. You could be arrested for this crime.

Here are three reasons why you shouldn't smoke cigarettes:

- Nicotine is highly addictive. Once you start smoking, it is very hard to stop, and smoking cigarettes causes lung cancer and other diseases. Tobacco- and nicotine-related diseases kill more than 400,000 people every year.
- Each day, 3,000 kids begin smoking. One-third of these youngsters will probably have their lives shortened because of tobacco use.
- Children who smoke cigarettes are almost six times more likely to use other illegal drugs than kids who don't smoke.

If your parents haven't told you how they feel about the dangers of illegal drugs, ask them. One of every 10 kids aged 12 to 17 is using illegal drugs. They do not understand the risks they are taking with their health and their lives. However, the vast majority of young people in America are smart enough to figure out that drugs, cigarettes, and alcohol could rob them of their future. Be your body's best friend: guard your mental and physical health by staying away from drugs.

WHY SHOULD I LEARN ABOUT DRUGS?

Steven L. Jaffe, M.D., Senior Consulting Editor,
Professor of Child and Adolescent Psychiatry,
Emory University

Your grandparents and great-grandparents did not think much about "drug awareness." That's because drugs, to most of them, simply meant "medicine."

Of the three types of drugs, medicine is the good type. Medicines such as penicillin and aspirin promote healing and help sick people get better.

Another type of drug is obviously bad for you because it is poison. Then there are the kinds of drugs that fool you, such as marijuana and LSD. They make you feel good, but they harm your body and brain.

Our great crisis today is that this third category of drugs has become widely abused. Drugs of abuse are everywhere, not just in rough neighborhoods. Many teens are introduced to drugs by older brothers, sisters, friends, or even friends' parents. Some people may use only a little bit of a drug, but others who inherited a tendency to become addicted may move on to using drugs all the time. If a family member is or was an alcoholic or an addict, a young person is at greater risk of becoming one.

Drug abuse can weaken us physically. Worse, it can cause

permanent mental damage. Our brain is the most important part of our body. Our thoughts, hopes, wishes, feelings, and memories are located there, within 100 billion nerve cells. Alcohol and drugs that are abused will harm—and even destroy—these cells. During the teen years, your brain continues to develop and grow, but drugs and alcohol can impair this growth.

I treat all types of teenagers at my hospital programs and in my office. Many suffer from depression or anxiety. A lot of them abuse drugs and alcohol, and this makes their depression or fears worse. I have celebrated birthdays and high school graduations with many of my patients. But I have also been to sad funerals for others who have died from problems with drug abuse.

Doctors understand more about drugs today than ever before. We've learned that some substances (even some foods) that we once thought were harmless can actually cause health problems. And for some people, medicines that help relieve one symptom might cause problems in other ways. This is because each person's body chemistry and immune system are different.

For all of these reasons, drug awareness is important for everyone. We need to learn which drugs to avoid or question—not only the destructive, illegal drugs we hear so much about in the news, but also ordinary medicines we buy at the supermarket or pharmacy. We need to understand that even "good" drugs can hurt us if they are not used correctly. We also need accurate scientific knowledge, not just rumors we hear from other teens.

Drug awareness enables you to make good decisions. It allows you to become powerful and strong and have a meaningful life!

Today's drugstore is a far cry from the traditional pharmacy of previous generations. Rows of aisles display hundreds of different kinds of over-the-counter drugs that people can buy without a doctor's prescription. Statistics show that 80 percent of Americans' medical care comes from the over-the-counter drugs they buy.

THE DRUGSTORE

The traditional corner drugstore used to be a gathering place for young people and often for adults. It usually had a soda fountain and sometimes a lunch counter. People relied on the **pharmacist** for information about drugs they needed or wanted. A person with an ailment could go to the drugstore and talk to the pharmacist, who usually recommended a medicine that would help ease the ailment.

Nowadays, large, self-service drugstores offer an overwhelming variety of drugs, many of which we can simply choose from the shelves without the help of a pharmacist. Other drugs can be obtained only through a prescription from a doctor. The ones we choose ourselves are called over-the-counter (OTC) drugs or nonprescription drugs. It is estimated that between 120,000 and 300,000 OTC drugs are available in the United States. Millions of Americans use them daily, each one spending an average of $62 a year on them. People rely on OTC drugs to treat a variety of ailments, from acne to warts. There are OTC drugs for headaches, rashes, fevers, cuts, bruises, indigestion, coughs, runny noses, dieting, and an array of other purposes.

Why So Many OTC Drugs?

Most of today's drugs were developed in the last decades of the 20th century. Before that time, drugs usually came directly from doctors, who made up medicines to treat problems such as fevers, coughs, sleeplessness, asthma, and even heart ailments. Often, however, these medicines contained painkilling but dangerous drugs such as morphine and heroin. Although these are **addictive** drugs, doctors and scientists did not know that at the time, and the drugs were not classified as illegal until years later.

In the second half of the 20th century, medicines such as antibiotics (drugs that fight bacterial infections) were developed. Vaccines that prevent polio and measles were introduced. And researchers continue to develop drugs to help prevent or cure cancer, heart disease, diabetes, and many other serious illnesses. Today, a tremendous number of drugs help doctors and their patients manage illness. So many drugs, both prescription and OTC, are available that they are regulated by the U.S. government through a special agency known as the U.S. Food and Drug Administration (FDA).

How Are OTC Drugs Regulated?

The FDA decides which drugs are available only by prescription and which ones can be sold over the counter.

The agency also decides whether certain prescription drugs have proved safe enough to reclassify as OTC drugs. During the past 20 years, more than 600 drugs that were once obtainable only by prescription are now OTC drugs. For example, the anti-inflammatory prescription drug called naproxen is now sold in drugstores under the brand name Aleve. Tagamet and Zantac, which were both prescription anti-ulcer drugs at one time, are now also sold as OTC drugs.

The FDA follows strict guidelines. The agency looks carefully at the ingredients in drugs and thoroughly tests them for safety and effectiveness. OTC drugs are those that the FDA considers safe and effective enough to use without a prescription. Because many people rely on OTC drugs to treat a variety of conditions, it is very important that users know what is in these products, what the drugs can and cannot do, and when they should be taken. For this reason, the FDA requires drug manufacturers to include detailed information on the labels or packages of all OTC drugs.

Labels on OTC products are different from those on drugs prescribed by a doctor. Most often, labels on prescription drugs don't list the ingredients in the drug, state the purpose of the drug, or give information about the drug's effectiveness. Instead, they list how much to take and when to take the drug. Warnings about possible **side effects** are included on the labels of prescription drugs. But in general, consumers rely on their doctors and pharmacists to give them most of the information they need about such drugs.

On the other hand, labels on OTC drugs are much

more complex because these drugs are more readily available and therefore more likely to be misused. FDA rules require manufacturers of OTC drugs to provide the drug's ingredients, purpose, directions for use, and proper dosage, as well as any appropriate warnings about possible side effects. Other rules require that manufacturers provide information about any changes in the product and about the way the package should be sealed, so that consumers know whether the product has been tampered with. OTC drug manufacturers must also include on each package an expiration date—the time beyond which a drug loses its full effectiveness and should no longer be used.

For many consumers, however, OTC drug labels became difficult to read and understand. One reason is that until very recently, they were not standardized. That is, the labeling format varied throughout the United States. For example, one manufacturer might put its OTC drugs' dosage recommendation last on its labels, while another might list it first. Often, the wording was complicated, or it was printed in very small type.

In 1999, however, the FDA began requiring new labeling on OTC drugs that not only includes simplified wording and readable type size but also fits a standardized format. All active ingredients in the drug must be listed first. Uses, warnings, directions, and inactive ingredients must also be included on the label.

What to Look For on an OTC Drug Label

Before you decide whether to use an OTC drug, remember two very important things. First, no matter

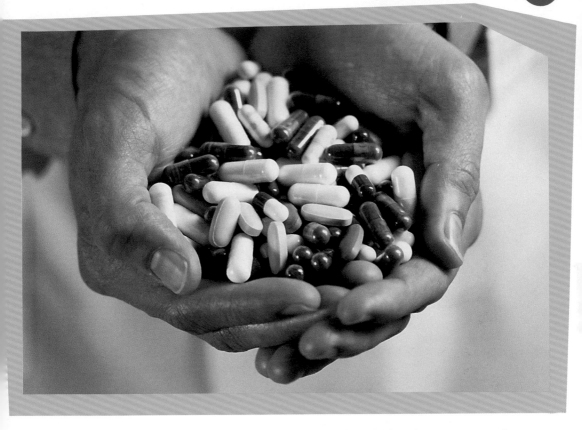

Capsules like those seen in this handful of OTC drugs were unknown until the late 20th century. Traditional medicines were usually tablets or syrups made up by doctors. People could also buy patent medicines—nonprescription "tonics" supposedly patented (licensed) by the makers. Ingredients in patent medicines varied widely and often included addictive drugs such as opium and cocaine.

how thoroughly a drug has been tested or how complete its label is, every drug has potential risks. No drug, OTC or prescription, is completely safe and risk-free. Under certain conditions, any drug can be harmful. That is why it is essential to read package labels. Second, keep in mind that OTC drugs only relieve the symptoms of an illness. They do not cure the basic cause of an ailment.

How can you learn about a specific OTC drug? First,

(continued on p. 20)

What's On the Label?

In 1999, the FDA required standard labeling for all OTC drugs. Manufacturers have six years (until 2005) to change their labeling so that the information is clearly readable and can be "understood by the average consumer." These pages show you what is on the label of an average OTC drug and tell you where you can find it.

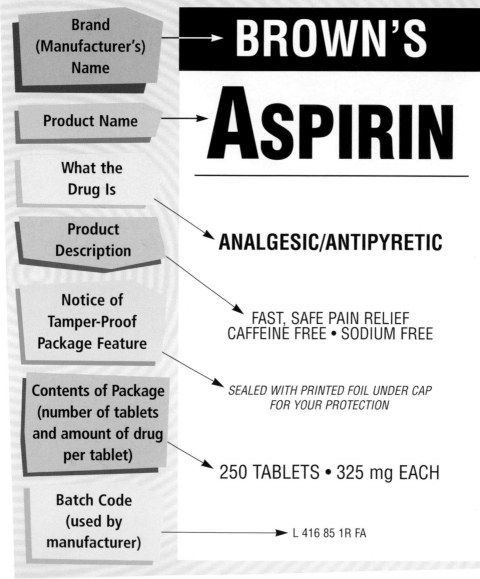

Brand (Manufacturer's) Name → **BROWN'S**

Product Name → **ASPIRIN**

What the Drug Is

Product Description → **ANALGESIC/ANTIPYRETIC**

Notice of Tamper-Proof Package Feature → FAST, SAFE PAIN RELIEF
CAFFEINE FREE • SODIUM FREE

Contents of Package (number of tablets and amount of drug per tablet) → *SEALED WITH PRINTED FOIL UNDER CAP FOR YOUR PROTECTION*

250 TABLETS • 325 mg EACH

Batch Code (used by manufacturer) → L 416 85 1R FA

BROWN'S
ASPIRIN
ANALGESIC/ANTIPYRETIC

FAST, SAFE PAIN RELIEF
CAFFEINE FREE • SODIUM FREE

SEALED WITH PRINTED FOIL UNDER CAP
FOR YOUR PROTECTION

250 TABLETS • 325 mg EACH

L 418 85 18 PA

What the Drug is For

How Much to Take and When to Take It

INDICATIONS: Fast, safe temporary relief of headache pain, muscular aches and pains, aches and fever due to colds, and minor aches and pains of arthritis.

DIRECTIONS: Adults, take 1 or 2 tablets with water every 4 hours as needed, up to a maximum of 12 tablets per 24 hours or as directed by a doctor. Children under twelve years of age: consult a doctor.

WARNING: Children and teenagers should not use this medicine for chicken pox or flu symptoms before a doctor is consulted about Reye's syndrome, a rare but serious illness reported to be associated with aspirin. Do not take if: allergic to aspirin; have asthma; for pain for more than 10 days or for fever for more than 3 days unless directed by a doctor. If pain or fever persists or gets worse, if new symptoms occur, or if redness or swelling is present, consult a doctor because these could be signs of a serious condition. Keep out of reach of children. In case of accidental overdose, contact a doctor immediately. As with any drug, if you are pregnant or nursing a baby, seek the advice of a health professional before using this product.

IT IS ESPECIALLY IMPORTANT NOT TO USE ASPIRIN DURING THE LAST 3 MONTHS OF PREGNANCY UNLESS SPECIFICALLY DIRECTED TO DO SO BY A DOCTOR BECAUSE IT MAY CAUSE PROBLEMS IN THE UNBORN CHILD OR COMPLICATIONS DURING DELIVERY.

Do not take if you have stomach problems (such as heartburn, upset stomach or stomach pain) that persist or recur, or if you have ulcers or bleeding problems, unless directed by a doctor. If ringing in the ears or loss of hearing occurs, consult a doctor before taking again. Consult a dentist promptly for toothaches.

DRUG INTERACTION PRECAUTION: Do not take this product if you are taking a prescription drug for anticoagulation (thinning of the blood), diabetes, gout or arthritis unless directed by a doctor.

ACTIVE INGREDIENT: 325 mg Aspirin per tablet.

INACTIVE INGREDIENTS: Carnauba Wax, Glyceryl Triacetate. Hydroxyproply, Methylcellulose, Starch, Tail. May also contain: Dicalcium, Phosphate Dihydrate, Microcrystalline Cellulose, Silicon Dioxide, Stearic Acid.
Avoid excessive heat (over 104°F or 40°C).

EXP 09/2000

Warnings

Special Warnings

Drugs to Avoid While Using This Product

Active Ingredient (provides the desired relief of symptoms)

Inactive Ingredients

Expiration Date

(continued from p. 17)

check to see that the package has a tamper-proof feature (usually a tight seal of some kind). Look at the brand name, which is the name that a manufacturer gives to a drug when it has been approved for sale. For example, Tylenol is one of several brand names for a popular pain reliever.

A drug can also have a **generic** name, which refers to the chemical makeup of the drug. The generic name for Tylenol and other drugs like it is acetaminophen, which is the main chemical in such products. To make sure that drugs are as safe as possible, the FDA must approve the generic name. Many OTC drugs are available under their generic names as well as under specific brand names. When sold as generic products, they are often less expensive, but because each drug maker uses a different method to manufacture drugs with the same generic name, these drugs can produce varying reactions. It is always best to ask your doctor or a pharmacist before buying an OTC generic drug.

The chemicals in an OTC drug are listed under its ingredients as "active" or "inactive." Active ingredients are those that help relieve the symptoms of an illness or ailment. For example, acetaminophen is the active ingredient in Tylenol that helps relieve pain. Inactive ingredients are usually different types of flavorings, colorings, preservatives, or binders (substances that keep the active ingredients together as a capsule, tablet, or other solid form). Some OTC drugs sold as liquids also include alcohol as an inactive ingredient. Consumers should read these ingredients carefully to make sure that the product does not contain substances to which they might be allergic or that could be harmful to them if they are taking another kind of drug.

As you read the label of an OTC drug, check to see what the drug is used for and the proper amount to take. Is the drug for a sore throat, a headache, or a stomach upset? How much should you take at one time? When should you take it, and for how long? Check for any recent product changes in the drug. Sometimes manufacturers change their products to make them safer or more effective, but they don't always change the brand name. This means that a drug can have new ingredients, even if its name hasn't changed.

Warnings on OTC drug labels advise users of possible side effects, such as drowsiness, sleeplessness, or stomach upset. They also tell you about any products that might interact negatively with the OTC drug. Consumers should also check the expiration date of the drug. After that date, manufacturers cannot guarantee that the drug will remain effective. You should discard any medicine— OTC or prescription—that has expired.

When it comes to taking drugs, more does not necessarily mean better. You should never take a drug for a longer period or in higher doses than the label recommends. Instead, if symptoms don't clear up, see your doctor.

As consumers, we have a responsibility to use OTC drugs safely. So it is especially important to learn as much as you can about these drugs. In the next few chapters, we will examine a variety of OTC drugs and discuss what they do and how they can help or hurt us.

Although colds and flu cannot be cured by over-the-counter drugs, such drugs may relieve the uncomfortable symptoms of these illnesses. A lot of tender loving care can also go a long way toward helping you feel better.

COLDS, FLU, AND ALLERGIES

E veryone knows what it's like to wake up with a cold. Your throat is scratchy, you are sneezing or coughing, your nose is stuffy or runny, you have a headache, or you have a fever. You feel miserable. What makes you feel so sick?

The Common Cold

What you are feeling are probably the symptoms of the common cold, so named because it is probably the world's most common illness. The basic cause of a cold is a **virus**, a tiny organism that can be seen only with a powerful microscope. Cold viruses enter the mucous membranes that line the nose and throat and attack their cells. More than 200 separate viruses are known to cause the common cold. This is why symptoms vary among different people, and why each cold you catch

may feel different from other ones you've had. This is also why researchers have a hard time developing a medicine that can cure the common cold.

Cold viruses can be easily passed from person to person. Sneezing and coughing sends small particles of mucus from a person's nose and throat into the air that others breathe in. One of the most common ways people catch colds is through hand contact. Someone with a cold might cough or sneeze into his or her hand, and when you come in contact with that person's hands or touch an object he or she has touched, the virus may spread to your hands. If you then touch your eyes, nose, or mouth, you can come down with a cold.

Most colds occur during the winter months, but it is not true that exposure to cold or wet weather causes colds. It is true that such weather tends to keep people indoors, where they are likely to be in close contact with one another, increasing the chances of catching a cold. School children, for instance, are especially liable to catch colds or pass along cold viruses because they spend many hours a day in classrooms with many other children.

Cold symptoms take a few days to develop, and when you do catch a cold, you simply have to let it run its course. Depending on the virus, a cold usually lasts from 7 to 10 days. If it lasts longer or if symptoms do not seem to clear up, it's a good idea to see a doctor.

The Flu

Flu, or **influenza**, is also caused by a virus. Most people think that a flu is similar to a cold, but it is a more severe illness and it comes on very quickly. Flu viruses, which are spread by coughing, sneezing, and even breathing, attack the lungs and the breathing tubes leading to the lungs. A person with a flu can have symptoms ranging from a runny nose to a fever. These symptoms are often accompanied by a sore throat, aching joints, and loss of appetite. A flu usually lasts about 10 days, and it should be carefully monitored. If it is not treated it can develop into a much more serious illness, such as pneumonia.

Allergies

An **allergy** is the body's reaction to a substance that it views as foreign. The "invader" could be a germ or a virus, but most often it's a substance such as dust, pollen from plants, certain foods, and skin or hair from animals, which the body mistakenly attacks. Depending on the **allergen** (what is causing the allergy), people may sneeze, wheeze, cough, suffer from itching eyes and nose, experience stomach cramps, or have diarrhea. Why are some people allergic to certain substances and others are not affected by them at all? Researchers continue to seek answers to this question, but no one knows for sure.

You have probably heard of the allergy called hay fever. Maybe you even suffer from it yourself. If you do, you probably know that hay fever is not necessarily caused by hay and is not a fever. It occurs in some people when they breathe in pollen from plants and trees that bloom during certain seasons, especially spring and fall. The body of a person with hay fever instantly reacts to these invaders by producing **histamines**—chemical substances that combat the foreign invader. Histamines dilate (widen) blood vessels and cause the vessels to secrete fluids. They also irritate the body tissues and cause the itchy, watery eyes, runny nose, sneezing, and wheezing that are major symptoms of hay fever. Histamines are also responsible for the symptoms of other kinds of allergies, like pet allergies.

How Can OTC Drugs Help a Cold, Flu, or Allergy?

Colds, flu, and allergy cannot be cured by OTC drugs or even by prescription drugs. But you can find plenty of OTC remedies that will relieve the symptoms of these ailments and make you feel better. Some products help clear up stuffy noses, sneezing, and congestion; others relieve coughing or clear up breathing. Still others help reduce fevers and relieve muscle aches and joint pain.

Decongestants

A cold or flu can be treated with a **decongestant,** which works by constricting blood vessels in the nose, throat, and sinuses. This reduces the swelling of mucous membranes. As a result, nasal airways open up and the cold or flu sufferer can breathe more easily. You can take a decongestant orally (by mouth) in tablets or syrups, or in the form of nose drops or nose sprays.

Most oral decongestants contain a chemical called pseudoephedrine, which helps to open nasal passages and also reduces the production of excess mucus. Common brand names of decongestants include Advil Cold and Sinus, Dimetapp Decongestant, Dristan Cold Maximum Strength, Sudafed, and Excedrin Sinus. Oral decongestants take longer to work than do nose drops and sprays, but their effects are longer lasting. It is important to know the ingredients of your oral decongestant, because some cause side effects like sleeplessness, headaches, jitters, and heart palpitations (rapid, abnormal heartbeats). Although pseudoephedrine is a stimulant (a drug that increases the body's activity), it usually does not cause these side effects if used as recommended on the package. Avoid decongestants containing a chemical called phenylpropanolamine (PPA), which has a higher risk of causing adverse side effects. You can find out whether PPA is an ingredient in a drug by reading the list of active ingredients on the label.

Nose drops and sprays also relieve congestion by constricting blood vessels in the nose and sinuses, but unlike oral decongestants, they act within a few minutes after the user takes them. Brand names include Dristan, Afrin 12-Hour, Vicks Sinex 12-Hour, Neo-Synephrine, and Vicks Sinex. The major side effect of drops and sprays is irritation of the nasal passages, but they can also cause a condition called rebound effect. This happens when a person uses them for an extended time and then stops. After being constricted for so long, blood vessels can suddenly open up again, and congestion returns. For this reason, you should not overuse nasal drops and sprays, and you should take them only when necessary.

Cough Relievers

How can you stop the coughing that often comes with a cold or flu? OTC drugs called **antitussives** help suppress (reduce) a dry, hacking cough. Other OTC drugs called **expectorants** help you cough up the mucus or phlegm that causes congestion. Antitussives and expectorants are sold in the form of syrups and cough drops. So many different kinds are available that it can be confusing to find the one that's best for you.

The major ingredient in all OTC antitussives is the chemical dextromethorphan (DM). DM works by calming the medulla—the part of the brain that controls coughing. Antitussives containing DM are considered safe and effective not only for adults but also for children, because most people who take them don't experience any side effects. Brand names include Robitussin-DM, Benylin-DM, Contac Jr., Children's Nyquil Nighttime Cold Medicine, and Triaminic-DM.

Once again, it's important to read labels carefully. Many antitussives combine DM with other chemicals that may produce their own side effects or that are not recommended for children.

The purpose of an expectorant is different from that of an antitussive. Expectorants dilute mucus that causes congestion so that the mucus can be more easily coughed up and eliminated from the body. Most expectorants contain the chemical guaifenesin—the only ingredient classified by the FDA as being safe and effective for this purpose—along with other ingredients that suppress coughs or act as decongestants. Expectorants containing guaifenesin have few side effects, but those that can occur include sleeplessness, stomach upset, and rash. Common brand names of products for children include Benylin Expectorant, Naldecon-DX, Nucofed Pediatric Expectorant, and Vicks Children's Cough.

Cough suppressants, which are usually sold as syrups, reduce coughing by calming the part of the brain that controls the reflex to cough.

Antihistamines

People can treat the symptoms of an allergy with a group of drugs called **antihistamines,** which block the effects of the histamines that bring on itching, sneezing, stuffy nose, and watery eyes that are typical of many allergic reactions. Antihistamines don't stop the body from producing histamines, however. This means that if you are already having an allergic reaction, it's probably too late to take an antihistamine. These drugs should be taken before symptoms occur, to prevent them rather than treat them.

Antihistamines are among the most widely used OTC drugs. In addition to allergy medicines, they are also found in many decongestants because they help dry out and reduce swelling of mucous membranes. Because they can cause drowsiness and reduce nausea, they are sometimes used in sleeping aids as well as in drugs that help relieve motion sickness. It is not wise to take antihistamines if you have to be alert, however. For example, riding a bike while under the influence of an antihistamine drug could be dangerous, because your reflexes and coordination may be slowed and you may not be able to react as quickly as you should. Other possible side effects of antihistamines include dry mouth, blurred vision, and constipation.

Brand names of drugs that contain antihistamines include Contac Day and Night, Benadryl, Tylenol Flu NightTime, Chlor-Trimeton, Sinutab Sinus Allergy, and PediaCare Night Rest Cold-Cough Formula. In choosing an antihistamine, it is important to know the difference among those meant mainly for allergies and those that help relieve other conditions. It won't do much good to take a cold medicine to treat hay fever, for example, unless the symptoms are very similar to a cold.

In fact, because OTC drugs for colds and flu as well as for allergies come in so many combinations, it is difficult to know just which ones are the safest and most effective or which are to be used for different symptoms. One of the best ways to find out is to explain your symptoms to an adult, especially a medical professional. An adult can also help you read the labels of these products and answer such questions as what the drug is for, how much and how often it should be taken, and how long it should be used.

Drug-Free Alternatives

Do you *have* to use OTC drugs to treat colds, flu, and allergies? No—there other ways to treat these conditions. Health-care professionals recommend getting lots of sleep and drinking plenty of liquids to help combat colds and flu, since these illnesses often cause **dehydration** (loss of body fluids). Water, juices, and steamy chicken soup are good choices. In fact, chicken soup has been a homemade cold treatment since the 12th century. When a cold virus invades the body, special white blood cells rush to the site to fight the infection. As they do so, they clump up, causing inflammation. Although no one knows why, scientists now believe that the old-fashioned chicken soup remedy can actually help relieve cold symptoms by keeping these white blood cells from clumping together and reducing inflammation.

For sore throats, some people find that gargling with a mixture of salt and warm water is soothing. Nasal sprays of salt and water and steam vaporizers also help keep mucous membranes moist. A hot shower or bath may help fight off the chills some people get when they have a cold or flu.

Most everyone agrees that the best way to fight illness is to prevent it. Cold and flu viruses can live for some time on doorknobs, money, and other surfaces. Avoid spreading or catching colds and flu by washing your hands as often as possible—before and after meals, after handshakes, after using public phones or rest

rooms, or after being in a crowded place. Also, keep items such as drinking glasses, telephones, and dishes very clean. If possible, avoid crowded indoor places during cold and flu seasons (fall and winter months).

Allergies are more difficult to control. You may need to see a special doctor called an allergist, who can identify the cause of your allergies and then "desensitize" you through regular allergy shots. But the process occurs over

The best way to treat the symptoms of colds and flu is to let the body use its own natural defenses against illness. Drinking plenty of water and other liquids, getting plenty of sleep, and eating nourishing foods can help your body fight off these infections.

a long time and can be expensive. Most people try to avoid the substances that they know cause their allergies. For instance, someone who is allergic to a certain brand of soap can easily change to another brand, and someone who is allergic to cats can stay away from homes that have them as pets. A person with allergies to certain kinds of foods such as dairy products can adjust his or her diet. If dust causes an allergy, it may be necessary to follow a stricter cleaning schedule in your home. However, allergies can also clear up by themselves. Children and young people often have specific allergies that disappear when they reach adulthood.

There is another line of defense against colds and flu. It is the body's own **immune system,** which works to protect it from germs and infection. It is a complex system in which special cells recognize and respond to foreign invaders, such as viruses and bacteria. These cells attack and destroy the invaders. Part of what makes people feel sick is the effects of this attack. For example, in colds and the flu, the cells' action raises body temperature, triggering a fever, which in turn causes you to feel chills and aches. The invaders can't survive in the high temperature, however, and the immune system "knows" this.

Although the human immune system does not "cure" illness, it is important that it stays healthy enough to guard the body from sickness. You can help by eating nutritious, well-balanced meals, getting enough exercise and sleep, avoiding cigarettes and alcohol, and staying away from dangerous and illegal drugs. These are healthy choices to make whether or not you use OTC drugs to fight colds, flu, and allergies.

It's a great feeling to look good. But many people are preoccupied with weight and dieting and ignore the most important requirements for staying healthy. By themselves, OTC diet aids and supplements will not make people healthier, and they can harm the body. The best way to lose weight and keep it off is to eat lower-calorie, low-fat, healthy foods and exercise regularly.

3

DIET AIDS AND SUPPLEMENTS

As a society, America seems to be obsessed with weight and with dieting to lose weight. In films, on television, and in magazine and newspaper advertisements, we see happy, smiling, *thin* people. These images promote the idea of being slim over being healthy. Millions of Americans are driven to "crash" dieting as the quick way to be thin—and therefore, they believe, successful. Books and magazines publish endless arrays of diet plans "guaranteed" to produce weight loss. And there are hundreds of over-the-counter diet aids and dietary supplements on the market.

What are these drugs? What do they contain? Are their claims accurate? And are these diet aids safe? Let's examine some of them and try to find answers to these questions.

Diet Aids

Diet aids and supplements are only temporary measures to reduce weight, and they can have harmful side effects. Permanent weight loss occurs when a person takes in fewer calories by eating less and by following a regular exercise program. Some people turn to OTC drugs to suppress (lessen) their appetites.

One group of drugs whose side effects suppress appetite are **amphetamines.** This type of drug is available only by prescription. In the 1950s, amphetamines were widely prescribed for such ailments as depression and tiredness because they stimulate the central nervous system (the brain and spinal cord), which governs the activity of the entire body.

But amphetamines are powerful drugs, and they can be dangerous. Users can develop a **tolerance** for them, which means that they require higher and higher doses to get the same effect they once got from a smaller amount. Users can also develop chronic insomnia (inability to sleep), anxiety, nervousness, and even depression. Once doctors began to realize the dangers of amphetamines, they stopped prescribing them as frequently. Today, amphetamines are used only under a doctor's strict supervision to treat certain disorders, such as obesity (extreme overweight), narcolepsy (a condition in which a person falls asleep uncontrollably during daytime hours), and attention deficit hyperactivity disorder, or ADHD, which is characterized by a short attention span and hyperactivity.

An abundance of other diet aids that suppress one's

These capsules of an "energy" pill called Magnum 357s were found by authorities at an elementary school. The ephedrine in these capsules made several fifth- and sixth-grade students ill after they consumed them.

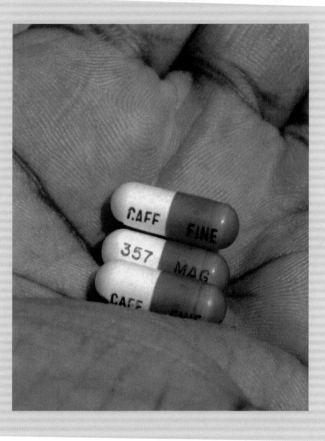

appetite are available over the counter. Many of these contain the drug phenylpropanolamine, or PPA, which is related chemically to amphetamines but has milder side effects if taken in recommended doses. PPA is the only drug that the FDA approves for use in OTC diet aids. Popular diet aids containing PPA include Acutrim, Dexatrim, Protrim, and Dietac. Researchers do not know exactly how PPA works, but they believe it suppresses the part of the brain that controls appetite.

Even when a person takes proper doses of PPA, however, he or she may suffer from dizziness, sleeplessness, or irregular heartbeat. Overdoses of products containing PPA can cause convulsions and raise blood pressure to dangerous levels. Since PPA is also an ingredient in some cold medications (see Chapter 2), a person who is taking a cold remedy should never use a diet aid containing PPA at the same time. Doing so could cause an overdose.

Because of the potential harmful side effects of PPA, the FDA requires manufacturers to put warning labels on diet aids containing the drug. Children ages 12 and younger should never use these products, and young people from ages 13 to 18 should not use such products without seeking a doctor's advice.

Another stimulant that can be dangerous but is nevertheless available over the counter is ephedrine. Derived from the ephedra plant, the drug has been used for centuries as a safe and effective treatment for asthma, and it is found in many OTC bronchodilators (drugs that relax the muscles surrounding the breathing tubes to improve breathing). When used without medical supervision or in high doses, however, ephedrine causes the same physical side effects as other strong stimulants such as amphetamines.

Despite the dangers, ephedrine tablets can be sold legally as weight-loss drugs—sometimes called "white crosses," "mini-thins," or "Magnum 357s"—because they are mixed with other substances and marketed as asthma remedies. The drug is also sold as a loose herb or tea preparation or as "herbal Ecstasy," which is incorrectly advertised as a safe alternative to the illegal drug known as Ecstasy. Because ephedrine is sold as a nutritional supplement rather than a drug, it is not regulated by the FDA. This means that the user cannot be certain of the quality or strength of the drug.

Although ephedrine is not presently classified as a prescription or illegal drug, it is a dangerous substance that can cause high blood pressure, strokes, heart attacks, and seizures if misused. Such reactions are so common that the FDA is thinking about putting tighter restrictions on the drug. More than 800 reports filed with government agencies describe the bad reactions users have experienced after taking products containing ephedrine. Another drug, pseudoephedrine (which means "false ephedrine"), is closely related to ephedrine and has similar effects on the body if used in high doses. As we learned in Chapter 2, pseudoephedrine is a common ingredient in cold, cough, and allergy remedies that function as decongestants. Drugs containing pseudoephedrine should be used carefully. Some people, such as those with blood pressure or thyroid problems, should avoid them completely. They should never be used as weight-loss drugs.

Stimulants are available not only by prescription and in drugstores but also in your local grocery store. Did you know that the caffeine in coffee, teas, some colas, and chocolate products is a mild stimulant? People use caffeine-laced products to help them wake up in the morning and to keep them going when they become tired during the day. Caffeine is also a mild appetite suppressant. And because it also functions as a **diuretic** (a substance that helps reduce bodily fluids), it is often an ingredient in OTC weight-loss products. But too much caffeine can cause restlessness, irritability, headaches, and irregular heartbeat. Caffeine is also habit-forming; that is, a person can become physically dependent on it for energy and alertness. If a person who uses caffeine regularly suddenly stops using it, he or she can suffer from mild **withdrawal,** a process that can cause physical symptoms such as severe headaches.

Some diet aids, such as Dieutrim and Protrim Caplets, also contain a substance called benzocaine. The drug, which is also an ingredient in so-called diet candy and gum, is an **anesthetic,** meaning that it causes a numbing effect. Its purpose is to deaden the taste buds in the mouth so that eating is less pleasant and the dieter eats less food. Although this sounds like a good idea for a weight-loss drug, scientific studies show that benzocaine is not very effective as a diet aid when used without other drugs like PPA. When taken in high doses or over long periods, benzocaine can cause blurred vision, dizziness, and confusion.

Diet Supplements

The most popular weight-loss products are OTC diet supplements, so named because they add to, or supplement, a person's regular diet. They include herbs, parts of plants, and substances extracted from plants. They may also include minerals and vitamins. Sold as capsules, powders, tablets, gelcaps, and liquids, diet supplements are widely available in health food stores, in drugstores, through TV commercials, and even on the Internet.

Although the FDA does not classify these products as drugs, it regulates them to insure that they are safe and properly labeled.

Diet supplements include fiber supplements like Citrucel, Metamucil, and Fiberall. These products are actually designed to be used as laxatives to relieve constipation, but they are sometimes misused as weight-loss aids. Once ingested, the fiber absorbs water in the stomach and intestines, which helps to soften and increase the volume of bowel movements. This often creates a feeling of "fullness" in the user, but that feeling doesn't last long. Also, laxatives and fiber supplements are not always safe for children to use, even for their intended purpose.

Other supplements used as aids to losing weight include "meal

Questions to Ask About Diet Supplements

Although the FDA regulates advertising for diet supplements, manufacturers often make claims for their products that are misleading or untrue. Here are some questions to ask yourself about diet supplements:

- Does the manufacturer claim that the product is a "secret" cure or a "magical" new discovery?

- Are vague terms such as "purify," "energize," or "detoxify" used to describe the product's effects?

- Does the manufacturer claim that it can cure unrelated conditions?

- Does the manufacturer claim that the product is backed by scientific studies, but lists no references to such studies?

- Are health "benefits" listed but not possible side effects?

- Does the manufacturer accuse doctors or the government of suppressing important information about treatment with the product?

If the answer to any of these questions is yes, it's wise to avoid using the product.

replacement" formulas and sugar substitutes. Many dieters use powders mixed with juice or milk to replace a meal, or they drink ready-made liquids such as Slim Fast. The manufacturers of these products claim that replacing one or two daily meals with a serving of their product will help the user lose weight. The powders and liquids contain substantial amounts of vitamins and minerals that a healthy diet can otherwise provide. But while meal replacement formulas are nutritional and can help users lose weight, the effects are usually short-term. Most people become bored with them and give them up, and many of them gain back the weight they may have lost while using them.

Drugstore counters often display certain weight-loss products as candy or gum. These contain the low-calorie sweeteners mannitol, sorbitol, or xylitol, which are considered drugs. Eating too much of these products at one time can bring on cramps and diarrhea, with resulting fluid loss. These side effects are especially likely to occur in children.

Eating Disorders

People who suffer from serious eating disorders battle daily with overeating, dieting, bingeing, purging, or starving (eating too little). One of the factors in eating disorders is one's body image—how a person perceives his or her body. Misconceptions about self-image can stem from outside opinions—what a person believes others think—but they also involve the way one handles one's emotions and attitudes about food. Although more females than males struggle with eating disorders, anyone of any age or sex can become afflicted.

Three major eating disorders are **bulimia, anorexia nervosa,** and **compulsive overeating.** Because any one of these disorders can cause serious health problems or even death, it is important to understand them so that you can recognize them in yourself or others.

A person suffering from bulimia eats large quantities of food at a time (binges) and then gets rid of, or purges, the food by inducing vomiting or using laxatives excessively. A bulimic person usually gets into a cycle of bingeing and purging that is difficult to break without professional help from a medical doctor or mental health expert.

You can tell whether a person might have bulimia by looking for signs such as these: episodes of overeating and then vomiting; hiding food; eating alone; feeling depressed or lonely; abusing laxatives or diet pills; experiencing physical changes such as dry skin, rash, or swollen cheeks; feeling weak; and having frequent digestive problems.

Anorexia nervosa (often referred to as anorexia) is much more serious than bulimia. Although an anorexic person may also binge and purge or may abuse diet pills and laxatives, he or she usually simply stops eating or drastically reduces food intake. The person may seem to be only "skin and bones" to others, but when an anorexic looks in the mirror, she sees herself as overweight. Anorexics may be high achievers who are eager

A Healthy Diet: You'll Like It!

The U.S. Department of Agriculture released a set of dietary guidelines that Americans should follow if they want to stay healthy and reduce their risk of getting certain ailments and diseases. Here is a list of what you should try to eat every day:

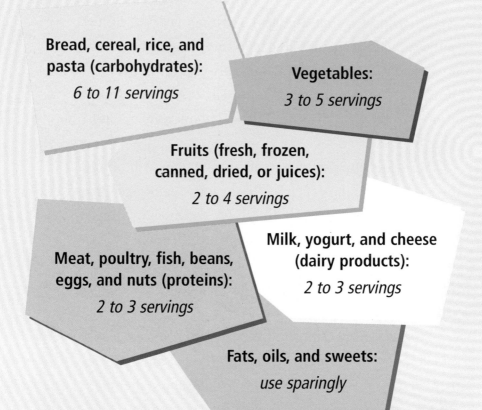

Bread, cereal, rice, and pasta (carbohydrates):
6 to 11 servings

Vegetables:
3 to 5 servings

Fruits (fresh, frozen, canned, dried, or juices):
2 to 4 servings

Meat, poultry, fish, beans, eggs, and nuts (proteins):
2 to 3 servings

Milk, yogurt, and cheese (dairy products):
2 to 3 servings

Fats, oils, and sweets:
use sparingly

Becoming health-conscious can help you respect your body and avoid the things that harm it. If you are exercising and eating healthfully, it seems a lot easier to say no to drugs and other harmful substances.

to please, but they usually suffer from feelings of low self-worth, anxiety, and depression. Denying themselves the "pleasure" of food is viewed as an achievement, a way to gain control over their bodies and their lives.

Like those who suffer from anorexia, compulsive overeaters are also preoccupied with food, but they focus their attention on eating more, and they often consume food to relieve feelings of anger, sadness, loneliness, fear, or stress. Compulsive overeaters frequently try crash diets, but because these diets don't change the overeater's basic pattern of eating, they usually result in a cycle of weight loss and weight gain. Like bulimics and anorexics, compulsive overeaters can also suffer from depression and feelings of low self-worth.

Good Eating Habits, Nutritious Diet

To lose one pound a week, an adult must take in 500 calories fewer than he or she normally consumes (about 2,200 calories a day). The best—and healthiest—alternative to using OTC diet aids and supplements for weight loss is knowing and practicing healthful eating habits. Following the recommendations of the United States Department of Agriculture's dietary guidelines (shown at left) is a good place to start.

Today, health-care providers believe that people don't have to suffer needlessly from pain. Although there is an abundance of OTC painkillers, some people also explore other avenues of pain relief that don't involve drugs.

THE BATTLE AGAINST PAIN

For centuries, people have been trying to understand and relieve pain. Aristotle, a Greek philosopher who lived in the fourth century B.C., believed that pain is an emotion and that people can stop pain if they really want to. Around the same time, however, a Greek physician named Hippocrates was using the bark of the willow tree as a pain reliever. In the Middle Ages, people viewed pain in religious or moral terms: as the will of God, as the result of demon possession, as punishment for sin, or as a sign of moral weakness. Since then, scientists have made great strides in understanding the medical and physiological reasons for pain, as well as in finding effective ways to control pain.

In general, there are two types of pain—**acute** and **chronic.** Acute pain lasts for only a short time but it usually comes on quickly and can be sharp or intense. For example, you suffer acute pain when you stub your toe, have a headache, or develop a toothache or an earache. You may also feel acute pain immediately after you sustain an injury, such as a broken bone. On the other hand, chronic pain is ongoing, long-term pain or pain that recurs frequently. Chronic pain often results from a severe injury or a disease.

Acute pain usually needs immediate attention. A toothache requires a trip to the dentist. An earache, severe headache, or sharp pain should probably be checked by your doctor. People with chronic pain have to find ways to cope with the condition. They may attend pain clinics, where medical professionals help them learn to control their reaction to constant pain. Sometimes people suffering from chronic pain also explore therapies such as massage, heat and cold applications, stimulation of the skin, and techniques for distracting them from the sensation. Often, drugs are combined with these techniques. Health-care experts agree that OTC pain relievers should be used only for temporary or minor pain. Severe or chronic pain should be treated by a doctor.

NSAIDs and Acetaminophen

Pain-relieving drugs are generally called **analgesics,** and scores of these drugs are sold over the counter in pill form. They have different brand names, but most contain one or more of five basic ingredients: aspirin (also called acetylsalicylic acid), acetaminophen, ibuprofen, ketoprofen, or naproxen. Of these five, all except acetaminophen are referred to as nonsteroidal anti-inflammatory drugs, or NSAIDs. This means that they block the production of prostaglandins, special chemicals that our bodies produce that are thought to be responsible for producing pain and inflammation.

Aspirin is the most common analgesic. Brand names include Bayer, Anacin, Bufferin, Ecotrin, Excedrin, and Ascriptin. Aspirin has other uses as well. It is an **antipyretic** drug, which means that it reduces fever. And because it is a NSAID, it also acts as an **anti-inflammatory,** a drug that reduces inflammation. Because aspirin's effects are so varied, it can be an effective combination drug to battle the symptoms of colds and flu. Aspirin also acts to "thin" the blood and prevent clotting, an effect that is helpful for people at high risk of suffering heart attacks or strokes. This is also why a person who has been severely injured and is bleeding should not take aspirin, since it may prevent clotting and make bleeding harder to stop. For the same reason, a person preparing to undergo surgery should not take aspirin.

Consumed in high doses, aspirin can cause dizziness and confusion. Aspirin overdose symptoms can include convulsions, rapid deep breathing, severe pain and bleeding in the stomach, hallucinations, and heart failure.

The most important fact to remember about aspirin and products containing aspirin is *never to give them to children and teenagers.* Studies have discovered a link between aspirin and the childhood disease known as Reye's syndrome, a rare but potentially fatal disease that affects the liver and brain. Because of this danger, healthcare professionals recommend other types of analgesics such as acetaminophen for young people.

Aspirin is one of the most well-known pain relievers. It has been used by medical professionals and consumers for about 100 years. Shown here is a bottle of Bayer aspirin from the beginning of the 20th century. Aspirin was first manufactured in Germany in powder form by the Bayer Company.

Acetaminophen is the major ingredient in the brand-name products Tylenol, Allerest, and Panadol Children's. It is a popular substitute for people who cannot or should not take aspirin. Acetaminophen products are very effective pain relievers and antipyretics, and they do not irritate the stomach the way aspirin can. Acetaminophen products are not NSAIDs, however, so they are not effective in treating the pain that comes from inflammation.

Although acetaminophen can safely be taken by children, it can create serious side effects in adults who take it in large quantities. Prolonged use or large doses may cause liver or kidney damage, and in some extreme cases sudden liver failure and death. And since many different kinds of cold remedies contain acetaminophen, it may be easy to take more than the recommended dose when combining these drugs to treat an illness. For example, the cough syrup or antihistamine you take for your cold may also contain acetaminophen. Symptoms of overdose often don't appear for several days, but treatment is effective only if it begins within 24 hours of the overdose. For these reasons, it is very important to read the label of each OTC drug before you use it.

OTC pain relievers containing ibuprofen, ketoprofen, and naproxen offer pain relief similar to that of aspirin. Unlike acetaminophen, they are NSAIDs. Brand-name products containing ibuprofen include Advil and Motrin IB. One disadvantage of ibuprofen is that it gives relief for only about four hours and must be taken several times a day. Another drawback is that, although ibuprofen is less irritating to the stomach than aspirin, it can cause stomach bleeding as well as headaches, dizziness, and drowsiness if taken in more than the recommended doses. Children ages 12 and younger should take ibuprofen only under a doctor's supervision.

Ketoprofen, the analgesic found in brand names such as Actron and Orudis, is the most recent FDA-approved pain reliever for over-the-counter sale. Like ibuprofen, it is short-acting, so it must be taken several times a day to work effectively. Like other analgesics, it can also cause stomach irritation if taken in high doses. It is not recommended for children ages 16 and younger.

The brand names Aleve and Naprosyn contain another kind of analgesic, the drug naproxen. Naproxen's advantage over other pain relievers is that it is longer lasting. One dose of naproxen can offer pain relief for up to 12 hours, so users do not need to take the drug as often as they would take other analgesics. Like most other pain relievers, naproxen is not recommended for children ages 12 and younger.

Topical Pain Relievers

A different category of pain relievers includes drugs known as topicals—gels, liniments, lotions, and ointments that are applied to the skin to relieve pain from strained or sprained joints or muscles. Topicals are also used by people suffering from arthritic joints, as well as insect bites and other skin problems.

Some topicals, called counterirritants, work by slightly irritating the skin, causing a sensation that feels like heat or cold. These feelings mask the greater sensation of muscle and joint pain. This type of topical is usually a combination of aromatic ingredients like oil of wintergreen, camphor, eucalyptus, and menthol, and is sold under brand names such as Absorbine Jr., Ben-Gay, Mentholatum Deep Heating Rub, and Therapeutic Mineral Ice. Because of the way they work, these products should not be used where skin is already irritated, broken, or scratched. And they should never be taken internally because they can be very dangerous. As little as one teaspoon of eucalyptus, for example, can be fatal if ingested.

Another kind of OTC topical is called a local anesthetic. Unlike counterirritants, local anesthetics block nerve impulses trying to reach the injured area and deaden the pain you feel. Benzocaine (used in some diet gums and candies to numb the taste buds) helps relieve pain from itching, minor burns and sunburn, insect bites, poison ivy, and mouth irritations when applied to the skin. It is found in brand names such as Lanacane, Orajel, and Solarcaine. A similar anesthetic, lidocaine, is found in brand names such as DermaFlex, Xylocaine, and Unguentine Plus. Although lidocaine can relieve the same types of pain as benzocaine, it is less likely to produce an allergic reaction. However, benzocaine is not as strong as lidocaine and so it can safely be used more frequently.

Topical pain relievers also include a group of drugs known as antihistamines. These include creams, gels, and sprays, with brand names such as Benadryl, Caladryl, and Sting-Eze. As we learned in Chapter 2, antihistamines work by blocking the effects of a chemical called histamine, which the body releases to combat problems like insect bites or contact with poison ivy. Histamine is responsible for the reddening and swelling you feel in the area of the bite or infection. Topical antihistamines should not be used for more than a week at a time, but when used according to directions they are very safe.

Another kind of topical pain reliever, hydrocortisone, also fights the effects of histamine. Unlike topical antihistamines, however, hydrocortisone prevents the release of histamine rather than countering its effects after it has been released. Although hydrocortisone is generally very safe, it should not be used on children younger than two years old, and should not be used continuously over long periods. Over-the-counter medications containing hydrocortisone include CaldeCORT, Cortaid, and Lanacor.

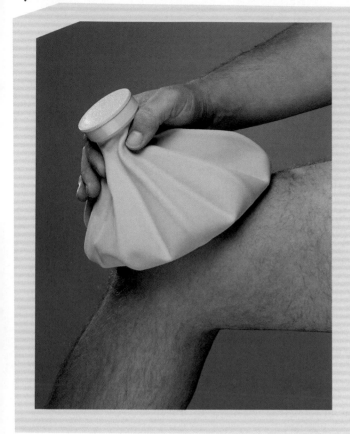

An ice pack is easy to use at home and is a good way to relieve pain from minor muscle strains and pain in the joints. Ice numbs the area around an injury and helps reduce swelling.

Nondrug Alternatives for Pain Relief

Many nondrug methods and remedies are available for people who want to treat their aches and pains without OTC drugs. One method relies on a substance produced by the body itself. Special chemicals called **endorphins,** which have pain-relieving qualities, regulate the body's response to pain and stress. For instance, when people exercise strenuously, they often feel a pleasant sensation rather than pain from overdoing physical activity. This is because the body has produced extra endorphins, which stop nerve cells from sending pain messages to the brain.

Hospitals commonly use heat and cold packs to ease

the pain cause by swelling, inflammation, and soreness. If you participate in sports, you probably have used this method. These treatments are safe and easy to apply at home as well. Cold constricts blood vessels in the painful area, reducing the circulation of the blood and helping to numb the pain somewhat. Heat opens up blood vessels to allow more blood to rush to the area and begin healing damaged tissues more quickly. Applying a cold pack first and then a hot pack not only reduces swelling but also allows increased circulation to relax and heal the injured area.

Many people choose to use home remedies rather than OTC products to treat minor pain. A witch hazel solution can relieve the pain of insect bites, cuts, and scrapes, for example. Bathing in warm water to which baking soda has been added may help ease sunburn pain, and the sap from aloe vera (a plant in the cactus family) can relieve the pain of minor burns. Small wounds may feel better after you apply a wet dressing of Epsom salts and warm water. A few drops of oil of cloves often soothe an aching tooth until you can see your dentist.

However you choose to relieve pain, remember that pain is a symptom of some type of illness, injury, or other condition that may need medical attention. Over-the-counter drugs and home remedies can help relieve those symptoms, but they do not provide a cure. If you have persistent or severe pain, you should always see a doctor or other medical specialist.

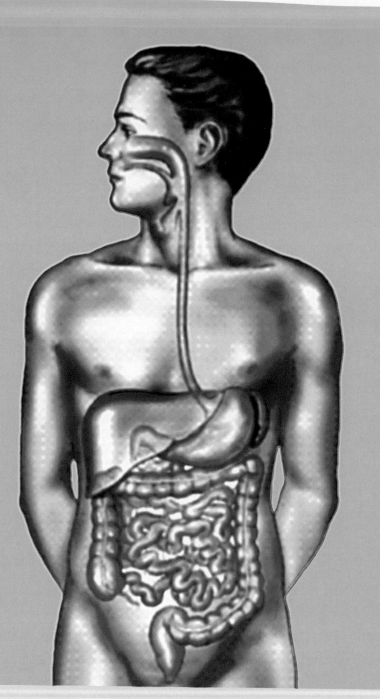

The job of the digestive system is to break down the food we eat into nutrients that can pass into the body's cells. If the digestive process is disturbed, fewer nutrients are absorbed by the body.

5

REMEDIES FOR DIGESTIVE PROBLEMS

What does the body's **digestive system** do? Its task is to break down the food we eat into components that can be absorbed by the body as nutrients. Digestion starts in the mouth with chewing; this is where saliva, an enzyme that begins breaking down food, is found. After food is chewed, it moves down the esophagus, the tube that joins the back of the throat to the stomach. In the stomach, different types of acids and the stomach's own churning action reduce the chewed food to liquid, which then passes into the small intestine. This is where much of the absorption of nutrients takes place. The remaining liquid then moves into the large intestine, where the water is reabsorbed by the body. Any leftover material, or waste, is passed out of the body as feces.

At one time or another, most people experience digestive disorders such as heartburn, indigestion, nausea, diarrhea, or constipation. What kinds of OTC drugs are best for these ailments? Let's examine some of the more popular remedies available.

Remedies for Stomach Upset

Heartburn, indigestion, nausea, and vomiting are considered stomach ailments. When the stomach produces too much acid, people experience indigestion, which is sometimes called "sour stomach." Indigestion can be caused by overeating or eating too quickly, or can even result from feeling excessive stress. Heartburn, a burning sensation usually felt in the chest, actually occurs in the esophagus when stomach acid backs up into it. For relief from stomach problems, the OTC products most people take are drugs called antacids.

Two kinds of antacids are on the market in tablet, effervescent powder and tablet, liquid, and gelcap forms. The two types give relief in different ways. One kind neutralizes, or counteracts, the acid after the stomach secretes it. This helps protect the stomach lining from becoming irritated and relieves the symptoms. Another kind of antacid was sold only by prescription until 1995, when the FDA approved it for over-the-counter sale. This newer kind works by stopping the stomach from producing excess acid. As a result, it can prevent the symptoms rather than relieve them after they appear.

Antacids that act as neutralizers include brands such as Alka-Seltzer, Maalox, Mylanta, Rolaids, Tums, Di-Gel, and Phillips' Milk of Magnesia. Most act quickly to relieve heartburn and acid indigestion by reacting with stomach acids to form a salt and water. The effective ingredients in these antacids are called alkalies, and they include magnesium salts, sodium bicarbonate, calcium carbonate, and aluminum salts.

It's important not to overuse these antacids, since the alkalies can be harmful in large doses. For example, Alka-Seltzer contains sodium, which can promote water retention and can raise blood pressure. Drugs such as Tums, Rolaids, and Maalox contain calcium, a mineral that strengthens bones, but too much calcium can damage the kidneys. And too much magnesium, an ingredient in Phillips' Milk of Magnesia, can cause diarrhea in some people. The aluminum salts in other antacids can keep the body from absorbing phosphate, another important mineral. In addition, all of these active ingredients can interfere with the body's absorption of other drugs, like antibiotics, heart and blood pressure medications, and thyroid medicine. People who are taking other drugs should avoid using antacids at the same time.

When people want to eat food that they know or think might cause heartburn or indigestion, they can now take antacids that prevent excess stomach acid from forming. These over-the-counter products include Tagamet HB, Zantac 75, Pepcid AC, and Axid AR. These kinds of antacids do not act as quickly as the neutralizers do, and because of the way they work they must be taken at least an hour before eating. Tagamet HB contains the ingredient cimetidine, which is the only active ingredient in the newer class of antacids that is known to interact with other drugs. For this reason, products containing cimetidine should not be taken with certain asthma medications, blood-thinning medicines, or drugs that control seizures.

No antacid should be given to children younger than age 12. And because antacids can interfere with the natural digestive process, it is not wise to take them over extended periods. Persistent acid indigestion or heartburn needs a doctor's attention.

Over-the-counter drugs called antiemetics can help relieve nausea or stop vomiting. (Nausea can also be a sign of serious conditions such as appendicitis, heart problems, and kidney damage, however. That's why a person suffering from prolonged nausea should consult a doctor.) For the kind of nausea that sometimes accompanies heartburn or acid indigestion, OTC brands such as Benadryl, Dramamine, and Bonine are helpful. These drugs also help relieve motion sickness, a condition in which the inner ear sends confusing messages to the brain. You may feel motion sickness, which occurs in children more often than adults, if you ride in a jolting car, on a whirling merry-go-round or other amusement park ride, or on a boat in rough waters.

One of the side effects of many nausea remedies is drowsiness. This is caused by antihistamines similar to those used in some topical pain relievers and cold and allergy medicines. In this case, antihistamines work by calming down the inner ear, which has become over-stimulated.

Remedies for Intestinal Problems

A common intestinal upset is diarrhea, which can be caused by bacteria, viruses, change in diet, or food allergies, as well as food poisoning or antibiotic medications. (While antibiotics kill bacteria that causes infection, they

So many OTC drugs are available for digestive problems that it is easy to overuse or misuse them. To find out which medicines are best for your symptoms, talk to a pharmacist or your doctor.

also destroy the bacteria that naturally occurs in the intestines and helps them function properly.) If you suspect that diarrhea is being caused by food poisoning or antibiotics, or if you suffer from chronic diarrhea, you should not use OTC drugs but should visit your doctor instead.

For temporary bouts of diarrhea, however, two major kinds of OTC remedies are effective. One kind works by absorbing excess water in the intestines, causing less frequent bowel movements. The other slows down the activity of the intestinal muscles so that waste passes through more slowly. OTC aids that absorb water include Donnagel and Kaopectate. Aids that slow intestinal activity include Imodium A-D and Maalox Anti-Diarrheal. A third substance that helps relieve diarrhea does not fit in either of these categories because it works on several different levels. Bismuth subsalicylate, found in the brand name Pepto-Bismol, works to normalize fluid levels and destroy organisms that may be causing diarrhea. A common problem with diarrhea, especially in children, is dehydration (loss of fluid), which can happen very quickly. To avoid dehydration, drink plenty of fluids, especially water.

Some people prefer natural aids to combat diarrhea, such as eating a mixture of carrots, barley water, and powdered cinnamon. Others try what is called the BRAT diet—bananas, rice, apples, and toast. It is thought that bananas help restore the body's proper level of potassium, which is necessary for strong muscles and bones. Rice helps to absorb excess water, apples provide fiber, and toast helps settle the stomach upset that may accompany diarrhea.

Another common intestinal ailment is constipation, which can be caused by poor eating habits, lack of fiber in the diet, or a lack of fluids or regular exercise. OTC laxatives, which are sold in bulk-forming, stimulant, and lubricant form, can help relieve this problem. There are scores of aids on the market for relieving constipation, and choosing among them can be confusing. Health experts, however, recommend bulk-forming laxatives because they mimic the way in which the body eliminates waste. These include the brand names Fiberall, FiberCon, and Citrucel, which absorb water in the stool and make it easier to eliminate. Bulk-forming laxatives are considered safer to use over an extended period than other types, although they can cause diarrhea and excessive water loss if not taken according to package directions.

Stimulant laxatives, such as Ex-Lax, Feen-a-Mint, and Dulcolax, increase the waves of muscle contractions in the intestines, speeding up the passage of waste. Taking a stimulant laxative for longer than a week, however, can cause severe or ongoing diarrhea. The third category of laxative, lubricants, includes brands such as Correctol, Ex-Lax Extra Gentle, and Haleys M-O. Like stimulant laxatives, lubricants, which soften stools, should be taken only for short periods, since they are not effective for prolonged bouts of constipation. One lubricant, mineral oil, may prevent the body from absorbing vitamins and may be too quickly absorbed by the body. Most laxatives are safe for children older than six if they are taken properly.

Although laxatives provide relief from constipation, the best way to avoid the problem is to include plenty of fiber in your diet. Eat bran cereals, fruits, and vegetables, and be sure to drink plenty of water every day. As with other OTC drugs, it is important to read and understand package labels and to carefully follow directions.

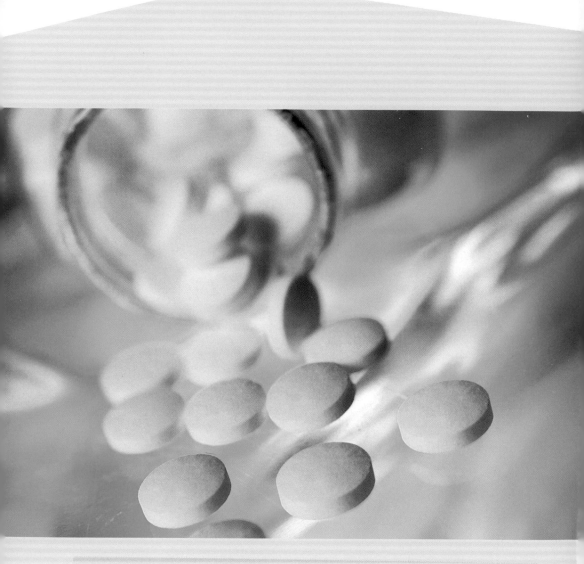

People want to look good on the outside and feel good on the inside. Many of us turn to OTC drugs and other products that help with skin, hair, and scalp problems. Other OTC products, like these tablets, can give short-term relief to people who have trouble sleeping.

OTHER OTC PRODUCTS

You want your skin to be smooth and spotless. You want your hair to be clean, shiny, and free of dandruff. And you certainly want to get rid of perspiration odor so that you smell clean and fresh. You also know that getting a good night's sleep every night is important for your health. Can you get these results from OTC products?

Aids for Skin and Scalp

The condition known as acne is caused when oil-producing glands and hair follicles in the skin become inflamed. The glands may produce too much oil, which gets trapped in the hair follicles and causes infection. Acne is most common in teenagers and has been linked to hormonal changes that occur during adolescence. It can also result from perspiration and from oils and other

Washing your face regularly is one of the best ways to help control acne. Another way for girls and women especially is to be careful about using cosmetics. Overuse of cosmetics can clog pores, as can oil and other substances from hair products. Another important way to help treat acne is to make sure pillowcases are always clean.

substances in cosmetics and hair products. Sometimes emotional stress can also bring on a bout of acne.

Many OTC products are available to treat acne. What works for each individual varies according to how severe the acne is and what type he or she has. Acne-fighting products are not a cure, but they can help control the condition.

Brand names such as Clearasil and Clear by Design contain benzoyl peroxide, which is very effective in killing the bacteria in hair follicles that causes infection. Brand names such as Fostex Medicated and Oxy Clean contain salicylic acid, which helps get rid of dead skin and unblock the sweat glands. Sulfur is an active ingredient in brand names such as Fostril, Sulray, and Acnomel. This type of medication reduces the amount of oil produced by the glands.

Acne affects 80 percent of young people, and although the condition is not a physical threat, it should not be ignored. Acne can be a source of embarrassment and emotional stress. Severe cases can also leave permanent scars. If OTC acne treatments do not seem to work, your doctor can prescribe drugs that may help.

If you suffer from acne, you can take other steps to help clear it up that don't involve using OTC or prescription drugs. Using plain soap and water often works just fine. Avoid excessive use of cosmetics and hair products, and keep pillowcases clean. You may have heard that certain foods, such as caffeine or chocolate, cause acne flare-ups, but this is not true, according to most researchers. However, these foods can worsen an already existing acne problem if you are allergic to any of them.

OTC products can also be useful in treating hair and scalp problems such as dandruff. The scalp naturally sheds skin cells on its surface, but when the process is speeded up the result may be lots of dry, scaly cells that often cause uncomfortable itchiness and are unsightly.

Medicated dandruff shampoos can help control dandruff. Brand names such as Head & Shoulders, Selsun Blue, and Anti-Dandruff Brylcreem contain sulfide and zinc, which are safe and effective in slowing down the shedding process. Other dandruff shampoos, such as Ionil and Neutrogena Healthy Scalp Anti-Dandruff, work by loosening dandruff so that it sheds in smaller scales and is less visible. People who suffer from severe cases of dandruff may want to try special treatments prescribed by a doctor.

Deodorants and Antiperspirants

With the onset of puberty, changing hormone levels may increase perspiration and create stronger body odor. The odor is usually caused by bacteria in perspiration. Deodorants, which are available in gels, powders, and sprays, mask such odors with perfumes and ingredients that decrease the bacteria's rate of growth. Some health experts claim that deodorants actually do little to stop underarm body odor. Because deodorants do not affect the body's functions, they are considered cosmetics by the FDA and are not regulated in the same way as products that are categorized as drugs.

Antiperspirants, unlike deodorants, affect the body's natural processes by reducing underarm perspiration, and they are therefore regulated by the FDA as drugs. Antiperspirants include brand names such as Arrid, Ban, Right Guard, Degree, Speed Stick, Mitchum, Soft & Dri, and Secret. Most contain aluminum compounds and an antibiotic agent. Most are also combined with a deodorizing ingredient that helps mask odor.

Antiperspirants can cause skin irritation, stinging, tingling, or burning. Sometimes using the product less frequently or switching to another brand helps solve the problem. You should also avoid applying them to wet, broken, or freshly shaved skin. If symptoms are severe, however, it's best to stop using such products altogether or switch to a deodorant.

Sleep Aids

Nearly everyone suffers from an occasional bout of insomnia—the inability to fall asleep or remain asleep through the night. It is estimated that between midnight and 3 A.M., an average of 20 million people in North America are awake and suffering from insomnia.

Insomnia can be caused by any of several psychological, physical, or environmental factors. Some people are "light" sleepers who are kept awake by noises that do not disturb others. Illness or pain, as well as anxiety or depression, can also prevent sleep. Sleeping in an uncomfortable bed or drinking caffeine-loaded drinks such as coffee, hot chocolate, or colas may keep you awake or prevent you from sleeping soundly. Another cause of sleeplessness is a condition called restless leg syndrome, which is especially common among children. It produces an unpleasant discomfort in the lower legs that often begins just before a person falls asleep. This discomfort is often described as a feeling of "pins and needles" or a burning sensation. The syndrome produces an irresistible urge to move the legs constantly.

Despite what many people believe, prescription drugs are not the way to cure insomnia. Many of them are addictive and should never be taken by children. OTC sleep aids, which include brand names such as Compoz, Nytol, Sleep Rite, Sominex, Tranquil, and Unisom, produce drowsiness because they contain antihistamines. But their effects are short-lived and

Getting a good night's sleep is essential to staying healthy and functioning properly. Keeping your bedroom comfortable, avoiding late-night snacks, exercising regularly, and keeping regular sleeping hours, even on weekends, are among the best ways to make sure you get the proper amount of sleep.

usually mild. People who have pain that keeps them awake can try a different kind of sleep aid that not only contains an antihistamine but also an analgesic. Brand names include Tranquil Plus and Unisom Pain Relief. Health-care experts advise that people who experience insomnia for longer than a week to 10 days should seek professional help.

The best way to treat mild insomnia yourself is to try to discover the cause. Try staying on a regular sleeping schedule by going to bed and getting up at the same time each day, even on weekends. Be sure to establish a regular, comfortable, quiet, and dark sleeping area. Exercising regularly often helps people sleep more soundly at night—but don't exercise immediately before going to bed. Avoid daytime napping, using stimulants, or snacking before bedtime. Many people think that watching television or listening to a radio helps them fall asleep, but in some cases, doing so may increase wakefulness.

Using OTC Drugs Safely

As you now know, it is important to learn as much as you can about OTC drugs that you and your family use. You can do this not only by reading the labels of the products you want to buy, but also by doing some research yourself. Anyone who has ever visited a drugstore or pharmacy knows how confusing it can be to choose from the vast array of OTC drugs that offer remedies for problems ranging from weight control to stomach upset to dandruff.

But as you have learned, drugs that are available without a doctor's prescription are not necessarily completely safe. Some have unwanted side effects. Others are frequently abused or misused. Some even have addictive qualities. And many OTC products should never be taken with other medications.

Over-the-counter drugs can provide quick relief from minor pain or injury, or they can help you look or feel better. But remember—even though OTC drugs do not require a prescription, they are still drugs. Choose them carefully, and always use them according to directions.

GLOSSARY

acute—very sharp or intense, or happening suddenly and lasting for only a short time.

addictive—causing physical dependence that requires repeated use to function normally.

allergen—a substance that causes an allergic reaction.

allergy—a condition brought on by the body's reaction to a foreign substance. Its symptoms include rashes, watery and itchy eyes and nose, stomach upset, and breathing difficulties.

amphetamine—an addictive stimulant, or a class of stimulants that includes this chemical.

analgesic—a drug that relieves pain.

anesthetic—a drug or other substance that causes a loss of feeling or consciousness to numb or block pain.

anorexia nervosa—a serious eating disorder characterized by an exaggerated fear of gaining weight, leading to near starvation, malnutrition, and excessive weight loss.

antihistamine—a drug that suppresses or counteracts the action of histamine in the body. Antihistamines are used to treat the symptoms of allergies and colds.

anti-inflammatory—a drug that reduces inflammation or swelling.

antipyretic—a drug that reduces fever.

antitussive—a drug that suppresses coughing.

bulimia—an eating disorder characterized by compulsive overeating followed by self-induced vomiting, laxative abuse, or diuretic abuse.

compulsive overeating—an eating disorder in which a person consumes food in excessive amounts.

chronic—occurring over a long period or recurring frequently.

decongestant—a drug that reduces swelling in the mucous membranes of the nose, throat, and sinuses and thereby eases breathing.

dehydration—a condition resulting from loss of water from the body.

digestive system—the system that breaks down food into chemical compounds that are absorbed and used by the body.

diuretic—a substance that helps reduce bodily fluids by increasing the production of urine.

endorphin—a substance produced in the brain that helps regulate the body's response to stress, pain, and other internal and external events that affect one's well-being.

expectorant—a drug that helps expel mucus by loosening it.

flu (influenza)—a viral infection that affects the respiratory system and can be easily transmitted from one person to another. A flu feels similar to a very bad cold, with headache, fever, cough, and muscle pain.

generic—not having a trademark or brand name.

histamine—a chemical produced by the body that is released during allergic reactions or colds.

immune system—the bodily organs, tissues, cells, and cell products, such as antibodies, that protect the body against infection or disease.

pharmacist—a person who is qualified to make and sell prescription drugs.

side effect—a secondary and usually adverse effect other than the desired effect for which a drug is taken.

tolerance—a condition in which the body requires increasing amounts of a drug to get the same effect once obtained from using smaller amounts.

virus—a particle of living matter that reproduces only inside living cells and can cause infection or illness. Viruses are too small to be seen with an ordinary microscope.

withdrawal—a process that occurs when a person who is physically dependent on a drug stops taking the drug.

BIBLIOGRAPHY

Brodin, Michael B. *The Over-the-Counter Drug Book.* New York: Pocket Books, 1998.

Inlander, Charles B., Sandra Salmans, and the People's Medical Society. *The Over-the-Counter Doctor.* New York: Cader Books, 1997.

Mitchell, Michael D. and Marvin S. Eiger. *The Pill Book Guide to Children's Medications.* New York: Bantam Books, 1990.

Murray, Michael T. *Natural Alternatives to Over-the-Counter and Prescription Drugs.* New York: Quill, 1999.

United States Food and Drug Administration (FDA) and Nonprescription Drug Manufacturers Association (NDMA). "Kids Aren't Just Small Adults: Important Information About Giving Nonprescription Medication to Children." Washington, DC: FDA, 1996.

United States Pharmacopeial Convention. "Guide to Educating Children About Medicines." Baltimore, MD: U.S. Pharmacopeial Convention, 1998.

———. "A Kid's Guide to Asking Questions About Medicines." Baltimore, MD: U.S. Pharmacopeial Convention, 1998.

———. "Ten Guiding Principles for Teaching Children and Adolescents About Medicines." Baltimore, MD: U.S. Pharmacopeial Convention, 1998.

Winter, Ruth. *A Consumer's Dictionary of Medicines: Prescription, Over-the-Counter, Homeopathic, and Herbal.* New York: Crown Publishers, 1997.

FIND OUT MORE ABOUT OVER-THE-COUNTER DRUGS

The following list includes agencies, organizations, and websites that provide information about over-the-counter drugs. Many national organizations have local chapters listed in your phone directory. Look under "Social Services Organizations" or your local guide to human services to find resources in your area.

Agencies and Organizations in the United States

At Health, Inc.
Eastview Professional Building
1370 116th Avenue, N.E., Suite 201
Bellevue, WA 98004-3825
425-451-4399
888-ATHEALTH (284-3258)
http://athealth.com

InteliHealth
960C Harvest Drive
P.O. Box 1097
Blue Bell, PA 19422
215-775-5155
http://www.intelihealth.com

National Clearinghouse for Alcohol and Drug Information (NCADI)
P.O. Box 2345
Rockville, MD 20847-2345
800-729-6686
800-487-4889 TDD
800-HI-WALLY (449-2559, Children's Line)
http://www.health.org/

National Families in Action
2296 Henderson Mill Road, Suite 300
Atlanta, GA 30345
404-845-1933

National Family Partnership
1159B South Towne Square
St. Louis, MO 63123
314-845-1933

National Institute of Child Health & Human Development
31 Center Drive, Building 31, Room 2A32
Bethesda, MD 20892-2425
301-496-5133
http://www.nih.gov/nichd/

Nonprescription Drug Manufacturers Association (NDMA)
1150 Connecticut Avenue, N.W.
Washington, DC 20036-4193
202-429-9260
http://ndmainfo.org/

United States Food and Drug Administration (FDA)

FDA (HFE-88)
5600 Fishers Lane
Rockville, MD 20857
888-FDA-INFO (322-4636)
http://www.fda.gov/

United States Pharmacopeia

12601 Twinbrook Parkway
Rockville, MD 20852
800-822-8772
301-881-0666
http://www.usp.org/

Agencies and Organizations in Canada

Ontario Healthy Communities Central Office

180 Dundas Street West, Suite 1900
Toronto, Ontario M5G 1Z8
416-408-4841
http://www.opc.on.ca/ohcc/

Saskatchewan Health Resource Centre

T.C. Douglas Building
3475 Albert Street
Regina, Saskatchewan S4S 6X6
306-787-3090

Websites

Consumer Healthcare Products Association
(Nonprescription Drug Manufacturers Association)
http://ndmainfo.org/

Consumer Information Center: Publications on Health
http://www.pueblo.gsa.gov/health.htm

Consumer Product Safety Commission
http://www.cpsc.gov

Council on Family Health
http://www.cfhinfo.org/

U.S. Department of Health and Human Services: Healthfinder
http://www.healthfinder.gov/

U.S. Food and Drug Administration
"FDA Guide to Dietary Supplements"
http://vm.cfsan.fda.gov/~dms/fdsupp.html

INDEX

PICTURE CREDITS

page
  6: Courtesy Office of National
     Drug Control Policy, the
     White House
12: AP/Wide World Photos
17: EyeWire MHE 050
22: EyeWire MHE 069
29: EyeWire MHE 075
32: EyeWire BEA 002
34: EyeWire BEA 039

37: AP/Wide World Photos
46: EyeWire MHE 013
50: AP/Wide World Photos
54: Corbis MED2031
56: NOVA ANATDT01
61: Corbis MED2023
64: EyeWire MHE 045
66: EyeWire BEA 049
70: EyeWire BEA 044

STEPHEN BIRD is a lawyer and author living in Canada.

B. JOAN McCLURE is a registered nurse and the mother of three children, ages 10, 12, and 14.

ELAINE ANDREWS (contributing editor) is a writer and editor of educational materials for children and the author of two nonfiction books for young readers.

BARRY R. McCAFFREY is Director of the Office of National Drug Control Policy (ONDCP) at the White House and a member of President Bill Clinton's cabinet. Before taking this job, General McCaffrey was an officer in the U.S. Army. He led the famous "left hook" maneuver of Operation Desert Storm that helped the United States win the Persian Gulf War.

STEVEN L. JAFFE, M.D., received his psychiatry training at Harvard University and the Massachusetts Mental Health Center and his child psychiatry training at Emory University. He has been editor of the *Newsletter of the American Academy of Child and Adolescent Psychiatry* and chairman of the Continuing Education Committee of the Georgia Psychiatric Physicians' Association. Dr. Jaffe is professor of child and adolescent psychiatry at Emory University. He is also clinical professor of psychiatry at Morehouse School of Medicine, and the director of Adolescent Substance Abuse Programs at Charter Peachford Hospital in Atlanta, Georgia.